Be Nice!

Be NICE!

*Discovering the pearls
in life's little lessons*

Saga Stevin

Gallant Press
Minneapolis, Minnesota

©2001 Saga Stevin. All rights reserved. Except for short excerpts for review purposes, no part of this book may be reproduced or transmitted in any form by any means, electronic or mechanical, without permission in writing from the publisher.

Gallant Press
    Contact: sagastevin@aol.com
    Check out her website at sagastevin.com
First printing.
Edited by Wendy Lukaszewski
Book design by Dorie McClelland, Spring Type & Design

Publisher's Cataloging-in-Publication
(Provided by Quality Books, Inc.)
  Stevin, Saga.
    Be nice! : discovering the pearls in life's little lessons /
        Saga Stevin — 1st ed.
    p.cm.
    ISBN: 0-9671612-1-5

    1. Conduct of life. 2. Benevolence. 3. Kindness.
  I. Title.

BJ1581.2.S74 2000   177.7
                          QB100-896

Other books by Saga Stevin:

*The Golden Triangle:
A Simple Philosophy on
Dating and Relationships*

and

*Power Walk:
Finding Supernatural Power
in Everyday Life*
Coming Soon

Be

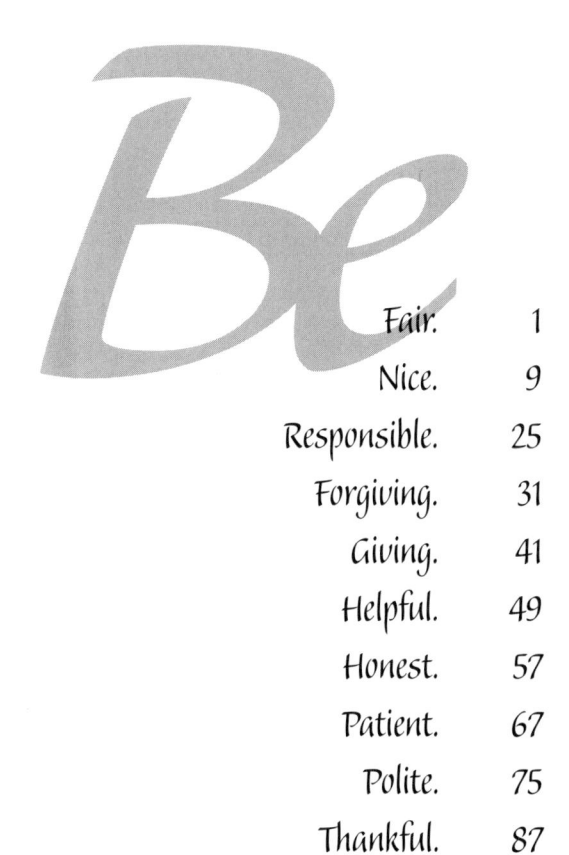

Fair.	1
Nice.	9
Responsible.	25
Forgiving.	31
Giving.	41
Helpful.	49
Honest.	57
Patient.	67
Polite.	75
Thankful.	87

The purpose of these proverbs is to teach people wisdom and discipline, and to help them understand wise sayings. Through these proverbs, people will receive instruction in discipline, good conduct, and doing what is right, just and fair. These proverbs will make the simpleminded clever. They will give knowledge and purpose to young people.

~ PROVERBS 1:2-4

Preface

*Be mindful of the effect your actions
have on other people.
What goes around comes around.
You reap what you sow.
Do unto others as you would have them
do unto you.
You get back what you put out.
You made your bed,
now you have to sleep in it.*

These sayings stem from a biblical spiritual truth. "Do not be deceived. God cannot be mocked. A man reaps what he sows."

(GAL. 6:7 NIV)

Be Nice!

This is such a simple thing. This is the crux for my writing this book. It is my wish that people would learn to be nice, polite, etc., so that their own lives would be blessed. In addition, these simple things would make for a much better world in which to live.

You cannot possibly think that, for instance, if you are lying and deceiving people to get what you want, be it a relationship, a job, a situation—it will last. It won't. All the lies will at some time catch up with you. When you lie and/or deceive to try to control or manipulate a situation, that situation will come back and bite you when you least expect it. People who do that, in trying to gain something, gain only empty and

Be Nice!

unfulfilled lives. These people will never be happy or experience any true sense of joy.

How can anyone think that causing pain in someone else for personal gain will lead to any kind of peace in their own life? Think about life in the big picture.

You have to be able to look at the big picture of life. You also have to have enough discipline and patience to do what it takes to live for the future. By that I mean to look at how your choices will affect your life in five or ten years. Also be mindful of how your choices affect the lives of other people. After all, the life you have is the culmination of the choices you have made.

Sometimes we think that if we can just manipulate a situation to get what we want right now—then all will be well. This is such a deception. It does not work to base a relationship (of any kind) on lies and deception. The relationship, or situation may last for a little while—but when it starts to unravel it ain't gonna be pretty. People are going to get hurt, and all because someone chose to be deceptive to get what they wanted at that moment.

Think about the seeds you are sowing. These are the seeds that are going to grow into the harvest you will be reaping. You cannot be a mean person and have a fulfilling life. You cannot be a deceptive person and have any true friends. You cannot be a rude person and have any respect. You cannot be a rebellious person and have any

Be Nice!

authority. You cannot be a controlling person and have any peace. You cannot be a stingy person and have any joy. You cannot be an impatient person and have any self-control. Without respect, self-control, accountability, thankfulness and patience you cannot have true wisdom. Without true wisdom you are no more than a fool whose life is folly.

So—if you strive to have a truly fulfilled life, follow the golden rule and sow good seeds.

Be nice, be polite, be forgiving, be good, be thankful, be helpful, be patient, be honest and be responsible. Then you will be richly blessed with a life full of joy, peace and love.

Be Nice!

Think also of the saying that the more you give the more you receive. If you live a life where your focus is more on what you can do for others, you will have a very fulfilled life! It truly is more blessed to give than receive. The truth is when you are a giving person—you really do get back so much more than you give.

Let those who are wise listen to these proverbs and become even wiser. And let those who understand receive guidance by exploring the depth of meaning in these proverbs, parables, wise sayings, and riddles.

Fear of the Lord is the beginning of knowledge. Only fools despise wisdom and discipline.

~ Proverbs 1:5-7
(New Living Translation)

Be FAIR.

To those who live in a world that glorifies "winning" at all costs, a "go for it" hyper attitude that doesn't take into consideration how their actions affect other people, the idea of being "fair" may mean a paradigm

Be Nice!

shift for many people. Even though we all strive for success and personal happiness—that is no reason to put blinders on the need to be fair.

Oddly, if we were to spend more effort on being fair, it would actually speed up the process of being successful. Perhaps also with lasting effects! This goes back to the spiritual law that you get more than you give.

Let's go back to childhood for a moment. Usually the first words out of the mouth of a child who is not getting his or her way is, "That's not fair!" Children are focused only on what they want now—not how it will affect others. Their primary concern is very selfishly motivated. The thought

Be Fair.

never crosses their mind how their demands might make someone else feel or how they will affect the overall outcome of a situation.

Sadly, a lot of adults never seem to outgrow this childish behavior or reaction.

The true spirit of fairness considers how your decisions and actions will affect the feelings, values and expectations of others—whether they are directly involved or not.

You have to be able to look at the big picture and realize the domino effect of how your actions do affect the lives of others.

Being fair means you take into consideration other people's needs. It means you forego making decisions based on what is best for you (alone) at that moment.

Put yourself in the other person's shoes.

Be Nice!

Better yet—ask the person (or people) who will be directly affected by your decision or action what they would consider fair.

This direct approach might take an ounce or two of courage for those who generally don't take other people into consideration. This course of action is always much appreciated and effective—whether it is in negotiating a business deal, squabble between siblings, or conflict in a personal relationship.

When you take others into consideration, you will find a great respect given you by others. You get this respect because you gave them respect. You showed them that their opinions and support matter to you—and that is what it means to be fair.

In doing this you need to always be

Be Fair.

open and honest. The more that people know about all the circumstances and factors that go into a decision, the more likely the outcome will be considered fair—for all involved.

You must be honest and open. If you are trying to manipulate a decision or situation by hiding, bending or omitting some or all of the truth, you will be setting yourself up for a big fall. Eventually the truth always comes out.

Think about if you had chosen the children's method of fair—the one that says "I want what's good for ME now!" Let's say you made a decision based solely on what you wanted or where you lied, deceived or manipulated in some way to get your own

Be Nice!

way. A decision that discarded the feelings, needs and effect on other people's lives—for your own purposes or desires. At some time the truth will come out.

When the truth starts to come out, all the webs you tried to weave will start to unravel. No one will have any respect for you. People will not support you or your future decisions or actions. People will not trust you or take your word at face value. You have created hard feelings toward people.

In essence what you have done is put a huge hindrance in your way of any kind of long-term success or happiness. You cannot build a future on a foundation of hurting, deceiving or defrauding people. Keep in mind—you did this to yourself. You created

Be Fair.

a world for yourself that will be empty and unfulfilled.

It may seem like a longer route to take other people into consideration when making decisions. It may seem like you are getting off track in your business or personal goals to always be fair. However, the truth is, you are actually speeding up the process by gaining the support and respect of others. You are creating a world for yourself that will be very rewarding and fulfilled!

There is a great inner joy in being fair—enjoy it!

Be NICE!

So many times I see and hear people around me complaining about their spouse/boyfriend/girlfriend—whatever. They tell me what they are doing, different situations that have happened—and their actions and

Be Nice!

words are so very cruel. People these days seem to have gotten into this warped habit of being outright mean to one another—and justifying their actions! "Well, he/she did/said this..."

Remember back when (perhaps in kindergarten) we were told to "be nice" and "if you can't say something nice, don't say anything at all?" Not to say you should stand by while someone abuses you—but this retaliation stuff has got to stop. All it does is keep mean behavior going in a vicious circle.

If someone says something mean to you—and you respond with something mean in return—on, and on that circle goes. The same with a rebellious attitude—

Be Nice!

they feed off of each other. The only way for the cycle to stop—is for someone to stop the cycle.

I know of so many married people who complain about their spouse. For instance, the wife will complain how the husband never does what she wants to do, always fights and contradicts her in front of the kids, and yells and calls her names. The husband says the wife will go out and do the exact opposite of what they agreed on, will leave him out of decisions regarding the kids, and doesn't care what his opinion is—she will do as she pleases when she pleases.

Both are rebelling against each other, not seeing their own rebellion. He/she is not doing what I want—so I'm going to do this!

Be Nice!

This is selfish rebellion run amuck and a vicious cycle that needs to be broken. The thing is, someone needs to stand up and make the commitment to break the cycle.

No one wants to be the first to say/do something nice to/for the other. There are all the "yeah, but's" going on. People—selfishly—screaming IT'S NOT FAIR! Both parties pointing fingers, blaming and accusing... well, you get the picture.

First of all, when you are married, you must realize you are both on the same side. Secondly, when you want to change a situation you have to change a behavior—namely yours. Being nice is not something you just try once or twice. Think of it as a diet. If you "try" not to eat that extra helping of key lime pie for one day—and you didn't lose

Be Nice!

those ten pounds you had set as your goal—does that mean dieting doesn't work? No. It means you didn't diet. It's not something you "try" it's something you "do."

The same thing holds true in being nice. It's not something you "try" once or twice, or for a week or two—it's something you "do" as a lifestyle—make it a habit.

Let me fill you in on a secret. If you start being nice to someone—their attitude toward you will eventually change. Gee—you could be starting a new trend. What a concept—starting a trend to be nice. When you think about it—what makes that so hard? Now it might take some practice, and some patience. But what a wonderful habit to acquire.

Oh, yeah—that pride thing. Well, there

Be Nice!

(pride) is something that will get you nowhere quick! Hold onto that pride—don't give an inch—keep on being nasty to each other...now there's a lifestyle to aim for! With that attitude you might as well go ahead and get a shovel because all you are going to be doing is digging yourself deeper and deeper in angst.

Look—don't expect overnight results—it took a long time to get into the deep rut you are in today. It will take a long time to repair the damage. Someone has to be the big, mature adult person and start. C'mon—take that first step. Go ahead—be nice.

It is funny how when you do something nice for someone, or compliment them, or say something nice, or apologize—how that

Be Nice!

will take the person back a few steps. It's like agreeing with someone. If they want to fight about something (that is a silly little thing that in the "big picture" really doesn't matter) and you agree with them—they can't fight you. It is impossible to fight with someone who agrees with you.

Most fights are about things that really don't matter anyway. As a matter of fact—most fights are about something entirely different than what is really bothering someone. Usually it is a strange game being played and really about all kinds of power struggles.

But, golly, work through the real problems. Then STOP nagging just to get your way—stop putting someone down just to belittle them. You have to give each other a

Be Nice!

chance to think and act on your own. There is generally more than one way to do just about everything. The only way to learn which way is best is to experiment. Something that may come easy to one person may not come as easily to another. It is also good to let someone discover for themselves how best to do something.

If you keep jumping on someone for every little thing, which, in essence, is trying to control their every move, you will eventually get one of two things: 1) That person will roll over and play dead—waiting for you to tell them every move to make because they are tired of fighting you; or 2) you will get major rebellion—that person will take so much then explode.

Be Nice!

If the person rolls over and plays dead you will end up complaining that they never think for themselves and you always have to do everything, or tell them everything. Can you see what is happening here? The fact that this is how you've "trained" them? This is exactly what you have taught them they must do to "make you happy." Only you are not happy. Now you want them to think for themselves. Whew—talk about running in circles!

The ones that rebel usually end up leaving or exploding and attacking. Then you cry "abuse" or "I don't know what happened!" And all for what? This is a reaction to the actions you initiated. This is the person screaming "enough is enough!"

Be Nice!

Give these loved ones a break. No one is perfect. To teach them to use their own minds—you have to let them use their own minds. Let them make some mistakes—that is how we learn. If they ask for your guidance—don't belittle them—give them a nice, gentle, answer—then let them make up their own minds to use your advice or not. Don't do the "I told you so." That is being smug and mean.

Being mean is a terrible trap to get into. Remember this—you reap what you sow. If you are mean and controlling and rebellious to those around you—how do you expect to be treated with respect and admiration?

Nurture—not torture.

You really do get more flies with honey

Be Nice!

than with vinegar. Observe the people who always seem to get other people to want to help them. They are generally polite, appreciative, gracious—in short they are nice. They treat people nicely.

You really do reap what you sow. You treat people mean... people treat you mean. You treat people nicely...people treat you nice. For the most part this is true. Yes, there are people who are just crabby to pretty much everyone. I'm talking about personal relationships. My guess is that people who have a basically crabby attitude are people who have painted themselves into a very lonely and miserable corner.

Again—it is all a circle. What goes around, comes around. Action and reaction.

Be Nice!

Remember—this world and the people in it are not all here to make sure you are "happy" and always "feel" good about every situation. Life is about learning to be flexible, and to have the courage to do the right thing.

Hey—I don't always "feel" like doing a lot of things—but I do them. And, I am better for it! That is called discipline. As for being flexible—it's kind of like doing the dishes.

I had some friends over for Thanksgiving. I cooked—they were cleaning up. They had been dating for about six years at this point. They both chose the task of doing the dishes. I noticed that they were trying to tell each other the "best" way to do the

Be Nice!

dishes. Of course I had my own opinion. You know—how to best conserve the water, which to do first (glasses, dishes, silver—pots and pans last, etc.). Then, instead of getting into a three-way power play—all of us knowing "my way is best," I took a deep breath and realized a great truth: It doesn't matter how the dishes get done—as long as they end up clean. In the big picture—that was the goal. I kept my mouth shut—and let them bicker. Finally the dishes were clean—but there was an unnecessary tension. It could have been a more relaxing time.

The same thing is true with carving the turkey. In reality, the goal is to get the meat off the bone and onto the plate. Think about that. What is more important? Getting the

Be Nice!

turkey sliced just so—or letting people enjoy themselves, the food and the company?

Maybe because of the power plays in most family dynamics and always having to be right, better or whatever—we have lost sight of what really matters. Gee—this could be the reason for all the family stress at the holidays.

We should learn to lighten up—and enjoy each other's company and the uniqueness of each other. Just because you always have a fresh turkey at your house, and you are going to your sister's house—where she got a great deal on a frozen turkey—doesn't mean it's the end of the world. It is fun to try turkeys prepared different ways—and corn bread—and pies. Hey—sometimes

Be Nice!

they are good—and sometimes they are flops. But learn to enjoy the people most of all. If the turkey is dry—drink some more iced tea. They probably realize it is dry too. Be nice and have a good time.

Life is not about who makes the best turkey—it's about who you share the turkey with.

What all this boils down to is being someone people enjoying being around. People enjoy being around nice people. If you can make someone's day by a nice word or deed—isn't that much better than ruining someone's day or hurting someone's feelings by being mean? So—be nice. And if you can't say something nice—don't say anything at all.

Be RESPONSIBLE.

Be responsible to people (not for people). In this time of self-gratification, people seem to be sacrificing compassion and responsibility for selfish, fleeting moments of irresponsible actions because "I have to do what feels right for me now." Well, here's a

Be Nice!

news flash: something may seem to feel right for you now—but if your sudden action has adverse reactions on other people, I can assure you—what you may think "feels" right for you to do is a setup for you to (continue to) feel empty and unfulfilled. You need to be responsible for your actions.

Being responsible means you are to be held accountable for your actions and decisions. To be responsible means, according to the *American Heritage Dictionary,* "capable of making moral or rational decisions on one's own and therefore answerable for one's behavior; capable of being trusted or depended upon; reliable; involving personal accountability."

Here's a big step up the maturity ladder.

Be Responsible.

You truly have to be accountable for your actions and decisions. This means you actually have to take into account how your actions and decisions affect other people.

I know life would be so much easier if all we had to think about was what we want, what we need, what can we get without a thought as to anyone else. Oh, yeah, greed rules! Except—what about the other people who think like that and won't they be stepping on our toes? Hmmm. Does this illustrate clearly enough the degenerate cycle of irresponsible behavior? A world where you can't trust or depend on anyone. A world where no one is held accountable. A world with a foundation and destination of death and destruction.

Be Nice!

Let me fill you in on a not-so-little, not-so-secret spiritual truth. A man reaps what he sows. We are all ultimately responsible and accountable for the life we lead and the decisions and behaviors we choose.

"Do not be deceived: God cannot be mocked. A man reaps what he sows. The one who sows to please his own nature, from that nature will reap destruction; the one who sows to please the Holy Spirit, from the Holy Spirit will reap eternal life."

~ GALATIANS 6: 7, 8

People count on you when you tell them you will do or take care of something. People count on you when you take a position to fulfill a task, be it personal or professional. When you prove to be an

Be Responsible.

irresponsible person it usually has resulted in hurting people's feelings, leaving people high and dry in a given situation, and losing the trust of people you know. This catapults you to live in a world (which you created for yourself) that is empty and unfulfilled.

If you are not responsible, happiness will elude you and you won't understand why. You will never have a sense of peace or joy in your life, will never be trusted by others, and will never have really true friends.

To create a life that is at peace and filled with joy you must be a responsible person. To have true friends, you must be a true friend—friends are responsible to (not for) each other. There is a wonderful life ahead for the person who is responsible.

Be FORGIVING.

Usually, a first reaction to being wronged is to retaliate. Most people get instantly defensive when someone says or does something that offends them—or something they interpret as offensive—or they hear some-

Be Nice!

thing from someone that so-and-so did or said that may have meant...well, you get the picture. You have to take into consideration the nature of the person. There are so many people who really don't have a clue as to how their words or actions affect others. These people are living in a dark place personally. They are people that seem to be mad at the world, or defensive about everything, or flat out don't understand. Some people just don't have the capacity for compassion.

Most of these people have very low self-respect, self-esteem, self-confidence—much less any people skills. Now, take notice of that last item. People SKILLS. To have a skill means you have learned and practiced

Be Forgiving.

something. Very few people these days learn what I refer to as people skills—how to talk to other people in a mature way. They haven't a clue as to how to have a polite conversation, to work through problems, to compromise, to see another person's point of view. So often it's about me—now. What I want without regard to anyone else.

This type of person probably doesn't have many friends because they are viewed as "handle with care." They may be seen as vain, self-centered, extremely dominant and highly volatile. People tend to "walk on eggs" around this kind of person and don't trust them or become too involved with them. Which in turn makes the person more of the above. It is a vicious cycle.

Be Nice!

The cycle can be broken—by learning people skills. By learning to look at other people's point of view—but mostly by honestly looking at your own faults—admitting to them and making an effort to correct them.

It takes a courageous person to take a serious self-inventory and ask for help to improve as a person. Baby steps—it's all baby steps.

So—how and what does knowing all that have to do with being forgiving? If you can understand the basic nature of the person who, in whatever way, attacked you, you may see that they don't understand how to communicate, or how to relate. They probably have no sense of compassion

Be Forgiving.

and truly don't realize the hurt they are causing. Generally, this type of person is so focused only on their wants they don't see themselves stepping on people to get what they think they want at that moment. This is precisely why you must forgive them—for they truly don't know what they are doing. They are so self-absorbed they haven't a clue as to the pain and hurt feelings and destruction they are causing others along the way. Which is totally different from malicious intent.

Keep this in mind—to be forgiving has little or nothing to do with all the possible reasons WHY someone has "done you wrong." This isn't about them. This is about you. This is about how you rise to

Be Nice!

the occasion and forgive them. Forgiving someone is for your peace of spirit. As opposed to holding onto a grudge or all the mean thoughts of how you can get back at, or hurt someone the way they hurt or humiliated (or whatever it was they did) you. If you don't forgive someone—you are the one harboring and dwelling on the ill feelings. This only irritates you. When you forgive someone—you let go of all the ill will and are free to move on with your life. That person needs your prayers—not your wrath.

The ability to forgive someone is a noble thing. The icing on the cake is how it gives your spirit a sense of peace when you realize (and stop dwelling on) the fact that most people don't know what they are doing.

Be Forgiving.

You need to accept them (as they are), forgive them (for they don't know what they are doing to you) and move on with your life.

When you move on with your life—you are all the wiser for being able to see past the person who doesn't have the insight to be mature and nice to others. In being able to see that—you will be more likely to avoid landing in those hot spots over and over again.

Remember—people don't know they are hurting you unless you tell them. People don't know they are offending you unless you tell them. People don't realize their words or actions are mean unless that has been brought to their attention.

You have no idea what went on in that person's life—or even what happened to

Be Nice!

them that day to judge them—or take their words or actions personally. You have no idea what event took place in their lives that caused them to become mean and hateful, or cold and callous. That is precisely why you should be forgiving.

This is not to say you need to continue to take their abuse. This is also not to say it is your job to be a social worker and try to "fix" them. This is just to say forgive them in your spirit, with understanding, and move on. Take yourself out of their way and do not allow them to harm you again.

Forgive them so you won't hold any grudges. Forgive them so you have a sense of peace in doing the right thing. All you can do is forgive them. Then you won't take

Be Forgiving.

the wrong done to you and spread it like a virus to someone else.

Sometimes when people are mad they take it out on those around them—most of the time people who had nothing to do with their anger—then those people get in a bad mood and take it out on those around them—see how this can spread like wildfire? Now—take a step back and realize that if you forgive the person—because they don't realize what they are doing—you can stop the cycle. This is a very good thing!!!

So—go—be nice, and be forgiving! Then you will be a much better person... and golly, maybe you can start to spread forgiveness and kindness.

Be GIVING.

I'm going to tell you something that on the surface seems to make no sense—but is one of the spiritual truths in life.

Be Nice!

The more you give—the more you have to give. Some know this as the more you give—the more you get. Then the more you get—the more you have to give. Sounds strange, but it does indeed work!

If you look around and take notice of the people who are truly generous people—it seems as though they always have plenty. On the flip side of that—those who are stingy or tight with their possessions are the ones who seem to always be at a loss in their lives. They never have enough—just ask them and they'll tell you so.

Sometimes, when we give something the reward is an instant look of surprise from the recipient—or an answered prayer. When you give of yourself or your resources you

Be Giving.

are giving so much more than the actual gift itself. You are also giving hope and faith. Faith in human nature—that there are good and giving people in the world.

It's funny how everything seems to go around. Like you get what you give. Know that someone is always watching you and what you do. I remember as a kid watching my dad pick up items that had fallen off the shelves in the grocery store and put them back where they belong. He also would always take his cart back to the front of the store instead of leaving it in the parking lot. To this day I do the same thing.

Kids watch parents all the time and emulate what they see. If they see their parents being stingy—they will be stingy. If they

Be Nice!

see their parents being rude—they will be rude. If they see their parents being giving—they will be giving.

Neighbors, friends, even strangers are always watching you. Like the old saying "character is displayed by what you do when no one is watching." Thing is—usually when you think no one is watching—someone usually is. Above that—you will know what your actions are.

It is also the little things in life. Tipping the breakfast waitress—overtip her and make her day. To add an extra dollar or two isn't going to change your lifestyle—and it will make her day so much brighter. Here is a good example of how you get back more than you give. The next time you go in to

Be Giving.

have breakfast—be assured that waitress will remember you and treat you extra special! See—truth in action—the more you give—the more you get—aside from the sheer satisfaction of the act of giving itself.

When you give with a cheerful heart, all things are possible. Some people think they are being giving when they give things with all kinds of strings attached. This is trying to be controlling and manipulating—this is not giving. A gift is something that comes with no strings attached.

If you give someone one hundred dollars and tell them that is to pay off a bill—that is not what I am talking about by being giving. That is trying to buy something. As opposed to simply giving someone a hun-

Be Nice!

dred dollars—period. They can put it in a blender if they want, or pay a bill or buy flowers—whatever they want to do with it. That is a gift.

Gifts do not have strings attached. Gifts do not come with attachments and requirements. Gifts are not things to be used to control or manipulate a person or situation. The kind of giving I am referring to is done with a cheerful heart. An attitude of "I want to do this" not "I have to do this" or "I'll do this if you do that." When you give freely with a cheerful heart—that is when you will be blessed with more and more to give. That is the cycle of getting more than you can give—so you can give more.

Be Giving.

Aside from that—it just feels good! So make someone's day—start a trend—give and be thankful for the ability to do so.

Be HELPFUL.

Which is harder—having to tell someone everything that needs to be done, or doing it yourself?

Some people seem to think if they say "just tell me what you want me to do and

Be Nice!

I'll do it" that they are being helpful. What you don't see here is that they mean, "I'm not going to do anything unless you tell me to do it."

People like this make everything a chore. Instead of—if you see something that needs to be done—just do it, they are making more work for someone by not doing anything unless told to do it. Let's use taking out the garbage as an example.

First of all, we can all agree that when there is no more room to put anything else in the garbage can—it needs to be emptied. To get technical, when it gets close to being full, it can still be emptied.

Now, if you have to tell someone every time to take the garbage out—it can get

Be Helpful.

very tiresome. It gets to the point you wonder if these people even have enough sense to come in out of the rain—or are they just plain lazy?

If you drop something on the floor—pick it up or clean it up. If you see the garbage can needs to be emptied—empty it. If you see the dishes need to be put away—put them away—and my personal favorite—if the toilet paper roll is empty—put the new roll in the dispenser.

Realize the fact that if someone needs to tell you every time, everything to do—that takes a lot of energy. You will create a lot of stress between you. The other person will either become an embittered nag, or shut down and just do everything themselves—

Be Nice!

and the lazy one will soon be gone. It takes a lot of energy to have to keep telling someone to do something, especially when it is the same thing over and over and over. Making someone do that is plain rude and mean.

It's kind of like if you see someone with their arms loaded with groceries, they drop something—and someone asks, "do you need help?" Of course they do—just help them—pick up the item and hand it to them. It's not hard to be helpful.

It is the smallest things you do that are remembered the longest and that mean the most.

Silly things like putting the emptied grocery cart in the cart space instead of leaving it in the parking lot. Picking up

Be Helpful.

that can of peas that was in the isle and putting it back on the shelf. Put the roll of toilet paper in the holder when needed—don't leave two squares of paper on there for the next person. We're not talking about major efforts or manual labor here, just simple helpfulness.

It's the basic lending a helping hand to a friend. Again—if you see something that needs to be done—just do it. Don't be one of those people who have to be told everything to do. Then you think everyone is nagging you because everyone tells you what to do. Hey—take some initiative, think for yourself, be observant—do something to help out.

If everyone would do what needs to be

Be Nice!

done, households would run a lot smoother with a lot less stress. Seems today though, that people are basically lazy and try to get out of having to do anything. They seem to want to see how little they can do—what they can leave for someone else.

Like drinking all but the last 1/4-cup of milk or juice so they won't have to throw the carton out—or make more juice. Does this seem silly and lazy to you as you read this? Think about the small amount of effort it would take to actually drink that last gulp and make more or let others know (by throwing away the carton) there is none left.

I don't know about you—but I really don't like it when I think there is enough milk/juice (whatever) to have a serving—and there are only drops there.

Be Helpful.

Be thoughtful, be helpful. Think how much nicer life would be if instead of trying to see how much we could get out of doing—everyone pitched in and did things as they needed to be done. Basically—if everyone were helpful, life would be so much more pleasant. And you'd be pleasantly surprised.

Doesn't it make you want to do more for someone when they do things for you? Here we go again—back to that circle. What you give, you get. If you are helpful—people will help you. That's nice.

Be HONEST.

This too seems like such a simple thing. Yet, there are people out there for whom this appears to be one of the hardest things you could ask them to do. These are the same people who think everyone in the

Be Nice!

world is out to "get them" in some way or another. What they, evidently, don't realize is that THEY are the ones who are hurting themselves.

People who lie—lie to everyone. The fact is these people cannot be trusted. Don't fool yourself into thinking that they wouldn't lie to you. At some point, they will lie or deceive you in some way—it's part of their nature.

There are several different kinds of lies. The lie of omission seems to be one of the most popular. It is a rather convenient kind of lie. It leaves the liar an "out" by saying, "well, that wasn't exactly what you asked," or numerous other word games. This can be

Be Honest.

very tiring to deal with because of all the ways it puts you in the position of having to carefully choose your words to cover every aspect of any given situation to correctly phrase a question so there can be no misunderstanding from a vague answer. Whew!

Deception is deception—by lies or omission. These people cannot be taken at face value. They cannot be trusted. Take what they have to say with a grain of salt, and watch the actions—which always speak louder than words.

People don't lie about what they are doing if they are proud of it and if it is the right thing to do. People lie to get out of responsibility, to get out of trouble, to make

Be Nice!

themselves seem like a better person, to avoid confrontation, to cover up a wrong, or to manipulate a situation.

If you decide to confront someone who is not an honest person about something you heard or saw that contradicts what they have told you, and their instant reaction is denial then attack, you can be pretty sure you hit the nail on the head. People who are honest can talk calmly about the discrepancy and will work to straighten things out. People who are deceiving you will try to turn the situation around and attack you to try to make you look like the "bad guy" for even asking.

It's not worth arguing or defending yourself to these kinds of people. They will

Be Honest.

always twist your words and turn them around to get the focus off of themselves. In doing this denial/attack dialogue they don't have to account for their deceptive words or actions. At this point it is best to let them go and get on with your life. These are not people who will be real friends.

Think about what a horrible life it must be to have no real friends, no one you can trust, and to drift through life from one bad situation to another. All this stems from the fact that "be honest" is not something practiced. The reason these people lie, or deceive, does not matter—they can always come up with a "good excuse." Not only do they drift through life with no real friends, they are also perpetually empty and unfulfilled.

Be Nice!

This is a vicious circle. To have real friends—you have to be honest with them. People feel betrayed when they are lied to. People know someone who lies cannot be trusted or believed. If you know someone is lying to someone else—you will always wonder if they are being honest with you.

Lies always catch up with you. At some point, they will always end up in your face. Then the liar tries to lie their way out of that too. So many lies—where do they end? With liars, they don't end.

Lies hurt people. Those who lie show a blatant disregard for other people's feelings. In many ways the meanest thing you can do to someone is to lie to them. Oddly, lying and being "brutally honest" are close cousins.

Be Honest.

When someone is brutally honest, they have no compassion for the other person's feelings either. Usually their "honesty" is laced with a mean spirit and is intended to hurt. It is all in the delivery—which is usually very backhanded. There is a gentle, compassionate way to inform someone of something or point out something you know is going to be hard for the other person to hear.

When people lie, or use brutal honesty to hurt someone, they are trying to control people and situations. Ain't gonna happen! That is exactly when the lies blow up in their face!

Keep in mind—you cannot control anyone or any situation. No one can control

Be Nice!

anyone else and no one can control every situation. You can influence other people—but you cannot control them. This is a hard concept for some people to grasp.

There is truth to the old saying, "it takes a genius to lie." Because you have to remember who you told what to. Talk about making your life so much more complicated than it has to be! Aside from the fact—if you are lying about something you are doing—that is proof positive that you know what you are doing is wrong.

The moral of the story here is to be honest. Simplify your life and strive to tell the truth. Surround yourself with good honest people and you will have a fulfilled life. Be a good honest person, sow good

Be Honest.

honest seeds and reap a harvest blessed with goodness and kindness. Let trust be something earned, not given away. Let actions speak louder than words and always keep your eyes wide open.

Eventually the truth always comes out, it's just sad when people get hurt along the way by a deceptive person. Choose your friends and confidants carefully. Be honest with yourself, with each other—you will have an easier and more fulfilled life.

Be PATIENT.

Good things come to those who wait.
Patience is a virtue.
It's all in God's time.
Let nature take her course.

Be Nice!

When I really want something to happen, I have a tendency to drive myself nuts with trying to force things to happen. Sometimes I feel as though I am spinning my wheels and wasting so much time and effort on things that are so totally out of my control.

A friend of mine once told me to look at my successes and learn from them. Funny thing was that my successes were all things that I did not "force" to happen. Usually when I would get ants in my pants trying to make something happen—it was a disaster. How many times do I have to put myself through this kind of turmoil to realize (again and again) that I need to let the situation go and pray it away? This is exactly

Be Patient.

when we need to lean on God and let Him take care of our situations.

Ah, yes... patience is a beautiful thing. Patience, according to the *American Heritage Dictionary,* "is capacity of calm endurance...usually through a passiveness which comes out of understanding...generally without complaint—though not without annoyance."

Pretty well stated.

Here is the part we need to understand: When we are in a particular situation that is not to our liking—it is human nature to force things/people to move or change to fit our needs at that time. When phrased that way, it does sound terrible. We really do need to realize that the situation is out of

Be Nice!

our total control and then hand it over to God. That is, after we have our prayer session and vent to the good Lord about our trials and how we would like for things to be. Then we have to be quiet.

We need to take a deep breath and be quiet so we will be able to hear God when He speaks to us. He will continue to place the right situation in front of us. We may not be able to see it—if we are bent on doing things our way, or are so single-minded about a solution, or not able to clearly see the big picture. This is also where faith comes in to play. God really does know what is best for us in the long run. Even He cannot force us to make the right decision or to take the opportunity presented to us—we

Be Patient.

all have free will. He can see things and knows things we have no ability to understand. Ya just gotta trust Him.

Let go and let God take over. When it is a decision or an opportunity from God, you will get a sense of peace about it. You will know the right thing to do—even if it doesn't make sense to you right now—He sees and knows things we don't have the capability to comprehend. Believe me—I am talking to myself here too—you are getting the benefit of my little reminder chat with myself!!!

So—I will trust God to take care of my little predicament. He does not give you gifts without the resources to take care of them. He will take care of the circum-

Be Nice!

stances. Maybe He needs to get you to a different place—and this is the route you have to take to get there. A no from God may just be a "not now." Maybe you aren't as ready as you think you are. Keep your eyes on the destination—and let God take care of the journey.

If He placed the destination on your heart and gave you the tools to get as far as you have gotten so far—He will continue to get you to the final destination. Keep in mind—as you get closer—the devil will try to trip you up so you will fail or quit. Be persistent in your destination, be patient on the journey. Don't quit just because you hit a pothole, and don't try to rush things just because you "can't wait."

Be Patient.

God knows the best timing for you. You need to understand that above all else. Once you have that understanding—you will have the patience to deal with the process.

God will give you a sense of peace for the journey. Don't give up—stay in the game and He will get you there. You will have to do the legwork—God will give you the tools—but you have to pick them up and use them. God did also give you a brain—and physical ability. Don't get sidetracked along the way and drive yourself (and everyone around you) nuts.

Have faith, press on and be patient.

Be POLITE.

This sounds like such an easy thing. And it really is—yet so few people these days seem to know the simple aspects of a well-placed "please" or "thank you."

Be Nice!

I was raised in the South, where we learned to say "yes ma'am, no ma'am/ yes sir, no sir, please, thank you and may I." We were also taught to call adults (especially our friend's parents) by Mr. or Mrs. and their surname.

These days I hear kids calling adults by their first name. I don't hear what we used to refer to as "the magic words." I don't hear, for instance, "please pass the salt." What I do hear is "gimme the salt."

There is a lot of "yeah" or "yep" instead of "yes ma'am/sir"—same with "no."

Maybe it's just me—but I do think the use of these more formal terms shows not only refined manners, but a bit of respect.

Be Polite.

It is such a simple thing to do. Such an easy thing to learn and teach. An unassuming habit that throughout your life will set you apart in a very pleasant way. Using these simple pleasantries will also cause people to treat you nicer as well.

It goes back to what goes around comes around—or you reap what you sow.

When you treat people with respect—they generally show you the same respect. The words you use are a reflection of the person you are. Don't you appreciate it when people ask for something nicely? When people thank you for the smallest things? When children speak respectfully by using Mr., Mrs., and Miss/Ms.?

Be Nice!

Especially as adults—you will see such a difference in people's reactions and willingness to help when you are polite. You can get far more accomplished by being polite in any situation.

Think about customer service. Whenever you have a complaint about a product or service—you call the customer service department to complain. The person you are talking to is not the cause of your problem. They really are there to help you. If you start off yelling and attacking them—how willing do you think they will be to go an extra inch for you? There is no reason for you to be rude, demanding or demeaning. Behavior like that will get you nowhere fast—and stressed out besides.

Be Polite.

The entire situation can be handled in a civilized, friendly, polite manner...usually to everyone's satisfaction, starting by using the "magic words." There is a reason they are called the "magic words." The magic that happens is this: people respond more politely right back to you. Try it. Experiment with your friends, with kids, with strangers, with the grocery store checkout person. Watch how people smile and respond positively right back to you.

Here is another thing to think about. When you are polite to others—you are actually setting yourself up to be treated with politeness. Here's how it works—what you give—you get. What you sow, you reap.

Think about the opposite effect. We

Be Nice!

have all run into, or know, people who are crabby or sour—and the last thing you want to do is treat those people with anything but that same sourness right back, much less go out of your way to help. You might even want to avoid those people all together. Perhaps that is why those people don't have many close friends...which is why they are crabby...which is why they don't have many friends...and round and round the circle goes.

Your attitude feeds off itself—either way—good or bad.

Now, I'm not saying you should be crabby and rude right back to those people—that will get you nowhere. Do not lower yourself to their level. Rise above the

Be Polite.

situation and continue to be polite. You don't want to be planting crabby seeds in the world. Keep planting polite and pleasant seeds and keep that good positive feedback heading your way.

Look, we all get in bad moods now and again—we all let harsh words and mean actions bother us. The problem is most of us then take out that hurt and anger on innocent people. The person who caused those feelings usually doesn't hear back about it—we usually take out someone being rude and crabby to us on someone else. Can you see how this behavior can spread and keep feeding off of itself from person to person like a virus? Take a deep breath, and be polite.

Be Nice!

Use polite words, whether you feel like it or not. You will feel better for it and you will help stop the virus of rudeness from spreading. Remember it is not "treat others how they treat you" it is "treat others how you would have them treat you."

Instead of letting crabby and sour attitudes spread, try spreading an attitude of politeness and respect. In a small way this will make the world around you a better place—which in turn will make the world a better place. I know this sounds overly simplified—it is the same concept of passing on the virus, only this one is a good, polite virus. It takes a bit more effort to be nice and polite—to rise above a situation and give back a polite word instead of retaliat-

Be Polite.

ing with a return volley of rudeness. Keep in mind—treat people how you would like them to treat you. Start a politeness virus and spread it everywhere—maybe it will be very contagious!

Wouldn't it be nice to live in a world where people really are polite? Where they asked for things with a "please." Where they responded for kindness extended with a grateful "thank you." Where when asked a question they responded with a "yes/no ma'am/sir."

The thing is—all you have to do is start living a life of politeness. You don't have to tell someone, you don't have to preach to people—just be an example. They will eventually catch on.

Be Nice!

Golly, seems a bit too simple, doesn't it?
Please use these words as often as possible:
May I
Please
Thank You
You're welcome
Yes ma'am/sir
No ma'am/sir

Be THANKFUL.

Here is a harsh truth for you: the world owes you nothing. Some people don't seem to understand this concept. They must think they are owed so many things because they are thankful for so little. Truth is, a little

Be Nice!

thankfulness goes a long way. An attitude of gratitude is a beautiful thing!

There is much to be said for the fine art of writing a thank you note. It is one of those things you really do for yourself. When you write a thank you note, or show your appreciation, or simply say thank you—you make the person on the receiving end feel much appreciated. This, in turn, leads them to want to continue doing whatever they received thanks for.

In some ways a thank you restores people's faith in other people. It also endears you to them. In every way it leaves the receiver with a good feeling when they think about the fact that the sender took the time to show they were thankful.

Be Thankful.

I try to always send thank you notes for gifts, which lets people know they are appreciated for what they have given. I also send thank you notes after being granted a meeting—be it for a job interview or to present a project. Once when I had a dental emergency and just showed up on my dentist's doorstep when he opened up—he took me right in, did what he could, then set up an appointment with a specialist for three hours later. He took special care of me. Yes, it is part of his job—but he went the extra mile. His thank you note went in the mail two days later. I was so grateful. After all—he didn't have to do all that he did.

People these days are so quick to complain and criticize—instead, it is nice when

Be Nice!

we compliment and extend that attitude of gratitude. This is another one of those things that gets passed on to make the world a little better place. Truly, the more you give—the more you get.

When you know that someone appreciates what you do for them, it prompts you to want to do more for them. I know there are people in my life who are so grateful and appreciative for the smallest things—that I so enjoy doing, and would do anything for them. On the flip side, there are people I know who seem to think the world owes them and think they should be given everything. Those are the people I have no desire to be anywhere near—much less go out of my way for or give anything to.

Do you see how being thankful creates

Be Thankful.

a circle of goodwill between people? Being thankful is not only for the person on the receiving end—it makes the giver feel good as well.

Sometimes people who are natural givers get tired of being unappreciated—then they will stop giving. For instance, my grandmother always sends checks in our birthday cards. For years she sent them to my brothers—never getting any acknowledgment (other than the canceled check) much less a thank you. Finally, she stopped sending them checks for their birthday. The sad part is she felt as though they didn't care about her. From their actions—she is right. A thank you note, or a phone call, what a simple thing they could have done.

You can't force someone to care, just as

Be Nice!

you can't force someone to be thankful. It should come as no surprise then when the givers stop giving to those who don't care and aren't thankful.

For those of us who take great joy in giving—there are always grateful people to give to. This is why there is the saying "don't cast your pearls before swine." When you have pearls to give—don't give them to those who will trample them. Save your pearls for those who will appreciate them and who will be truly thankful.

It is such a joy to be thankful, and there are many things to be thankful for. For instance, here in Minnesota when it snows (and it can really snow) I will be out shoveling my driveway for the third time in a

Be Thankful.

day, taking the quiet time to be thankful I didn't have to shovel some of my friend's driveways. Theirs are about three times as big. I am also thankful God gave me the strength of body to be able to shovel. Additionally, I am thankful for the quiet time while shoveling to enjoy the fresh air and have some God time.

Whenever you sit down to eat a meal—be thankful for the food in front of you. Give thanks to God for making all the wonderful things we get to eat. When I have my waffles in the mornings and I have strawberries and bananas on them I am so very thankful God made strawberries and bananas—they are wonderful! Let Him know how much you enjoy all He has done

Be Nice!

for you and you will realize how truly blessed you are.

It is the little things and it is the big things—in reality—it is everything. Be consciously thankful for what you have. Thank people for what they do for you and thank God for what He has done for you and how many blessings He has given you in your life.

Conclusion

Sometimes we think of these simple thoughts and behaviors as so easy. Well, they are easy to say—be nice, be polite, be forgiving, etc. And we think we are doing these for other people. The thing is, we are truly doing these things for ourselves.

When we forgive others—we let go of the anger and bitterness inside of ourselves. When we are nice and do the right thing—no matter how hard it may be at the time—we gain a sense of self-esteem. When we are thankful it fills us with an appreciation of even the little things in life.

So, in abiding by these "be attitudes"

Be Nice!

you are the one who truly gains in life. The added bonus is how these attitudes affect other people. You will also notice that in letting go of the vindictive, rebellious, selfish, bitter, nasty attitudes—you may also notice yourself becoming physically healthier—gaining a sense of inner peace and becoming a richer person in spirit.

This goes back to the golden rule and spiritual law. Following the golden rule means to treat people as you would have them treat you. Notice it does not state to treat people as they have treated you—no retaliation here. You are to treat them as you would like to be treated yourself. This goes hand in hand with the spiritual law of reaping and sowing.

Conclusion

You will reap what you sow. If you are rude and nasty, treat people with disdain and deception—then that is exactly what you will get back in your life. One of the ways you get this back is in all that negative energy eating at you. You will feed this and sure enough—it will grow inside of you. It is a vicious cycle that you have created and that eats away at you—body, soul and spirit.

You cannot have any sense of peace in your life if you are harboring ill will toward someone. You will always be thinking that everyone is out to get you. There will be a constant battle in your mind. You will never be able to experience true joy or peace when you choose to focus on things evil, hurtful, and bitter toward others.

Be Nice!

It takes a strong person to rise to the occasion and be nice, and it is this person who will have peace and joy in their heart. Doing the right thing is usually not the easy thing—but always the most rewarding thing. Like anything—the more you do this—the easier it becomes.

Saga Stevin,

author of *The Golden Triangle: A Simple Philosophy on Dating & Relationships,* is a personal-life coach and a public speaker. Among her many accomplishments, she has hosted a radio talk show and worked behind the scenes of several film and TV productions from Florida to California. Saga now lives in the Minneapolis area where she balances her writing and speaking schedule with riding her beloved horses.

Here's what people are saying about

*The Golden Triangle:
A Simple Philosophy on
Dating and Relationships*

"It is at once profound, funny, interesting, and inspiring! Saga Stevin has discovered the secret to healthy relationships: with self, others, and God."

~ Dr. Garrett W. Sheldon
author of *What Would Jesus Do?*

"A Godly, easy to read, much-needed handbook. *The Golden Triangle* should be required reading for every Christian single who is interested in living in the center of God's will."

~ Bill Myers
author of *Fire of Heaven*

With a 5-star rating, the reviews are in from Amazon.com!

Jane K. Brasovan from Houston, Texas:
This book presents a forthright correlation between the dating/relationship scene and God's Word. A must read for all singles looking for that "meaningful" relationship leading to a lasting marriage. Ms. Stevin has hit the nail right on the head with this one! All teen/singles organizations need to order quantities for their members to study. A greatly needed guide in today's society.

R. Hove from Minneapolis, Minnesota:
I read this book even though I feel that I am in a healthy, loving relationship. The book prompted discussion that deepened the way my significant other and I feel for each other, and the biblical references add a stronger meaning to the text. Also, Ms. Stevin's prose is easily read and understood.

M Hainje from Maple Grove, Minnesota:
Saga Stevin's style is warm and engaging, a lot like sitting down for a heart-to-heart with a best friend. And just like a best friend who tells it like it is, she lays out the truth according to the Source, God's Word. This is must reading for singles of all ages who desire God's best in their lives and relationships with the opposite sex.

From around the world people e-mail me about my book—here is a sampling of what they are saying:

It seems you have a great handle on many of the things that seem to puzzle so many people in dating/marriage/etc. I wish I could have read some of those things many years ago—it would have saved many mistakes and tears! **H.J.**

I am a Professor ... and teach Psychology and related subjects. In my classes, I talk about relationships and how men and women think and act differently. You certainly say it so much better. **F.P.**

Even though I am widowed, the book still was so beneficial to me. When we get to the place where we can't learn, we are in bad shape. If I ever marry again, I plan to put some of the things she writes about into use. **B.D.B.**

Coming soon by Saga Stevin:

Power Walk: Finding Supernatural Power in Everyday Life

None of us can control what life throws our way—good or bad. Nor can we help but make mistakes along the way. That's all part of being human. How we deal with these events, including the decisions we make, and the path we choose to take, are what is revealed in *Power Walk*. This is a very personal series of real-life events, describing how the author discovered the power of walking with God, and the healing power it has brought to her everyday life. It is a power that is available to all of us, and this book will tell you how to bring it into your life too.